Stay on Target

Stay on Target

Making the Most of Your Time

First published 2002
Copyright © 2002 by Moshe Goldberger
                                    P. O. Box 82
                                    Staten Island, NY 10309
                                    718-948-2548
ISBN 1-56871-226-X

Published by:
TARGUM PRESS, INC.
22700 W. Eleven Mile Rd.
Southfield, MI 48034
E-mail: targum@netvision.net.il
Fax: 888-298-9992
www.targum.com

Distributed by:
FELDHEIM PUBLISHERS
202 Airport Executive Park
Nanuet, NY 10954

Printed in Israel

With thanks to:

Rabbi Menachem Goldman

Mordechai Kairey

Charlie Mamiye

Binyamin Siegel

Dr. J. Cohen

Dr. F. Glatter

and others

Dedicated
In honor our children

Sarah,
Molly,
and
Joshua

by
Arlynn and Daniel Bock

Contents

Introduction

Why are we in this world? The answer to this question can be summed up by one concept: We are here to sanctify Hashem's name. This can be accomplished by spending each moment doing what Hashem wants from us at that moment. "Days are like pages in a book; inscribe in them that which you want to be remembered for" (*Chovos HaLevavos, Cheshbon* 11).

We express our thanks daily to Hashem "who changes the times and alters the seasons" (*maariv* prayer). A look at the luminaries which cause the times and seasons will help us understand the world and our purpose in it.

When the Torah teaches us about how Hashem created the world, we are given a list of six purposes for the sun and the moon: 1) to divide between day and night, 2) for signs, 3) for appointed times, 4) for days, 5) for years, and 6) to give light (*Bereishis* 1:14–15).

1. To divide between day and night: Without the rotation of the earth, which causes day and night, sunlight would deplete the soil's resources. Nighttime allows the soil to recuperate. People also have time to rest and renew themselves. The rising sun reminds us of the need to rise and serve Hashem with our daytime activities.

2. For signs: The moon is a sign that the Jewish nation will be renewed with redemption. The sun is a sign of Hashem's power. "If we cannot look into the sun, how can we expect to see Hashem?" (*Chullin* 60b). "The sun and the moon declare Hashem's glory" (*Tehillim* 19:2). "Lift your eyes and see who created these" (*Yeshayah* 40:26).

3. For appointed times: The luminaries serve as a calendar so that we will know when to celebrate our meeting days with Hashem — the *yamim tovim.*

4. For days: A new day helps us start fresh with new understanding, courage, and desire. We gain more each day of life; as we learn more about Hashem, we come closer to Him. It is imperative for us to note the passage of time in order to utilize our days properly (Rav Avigdor Miller, *The Beginning*, p. 32).

5. For years: The cycle of years provides the opportunity to repent of our sins and to resolve to improve for the new year. It also causes a circuit of *yamim tovim*, which are opportunities to review the great lessons of life and to understand them more deeply each time around. Hashem wants us to be happy with the seasons and to learn these lessons.

6. To give light: Sunlight is the energy source of light, heat, and all growth. Light also enables us to see and recognize Hashem's creations. Without the sun, we would have less desire to go through the day and accomplish things. Thus, the sun enables us to use our time properly.

How can we make the most of our time? Using the Torah's lessons as our guides, we will explore different facets of our daily lives and learn how to make every minute count in order to achieve our goals. Although our time on earth is limited, every moment can be utilized to sanctify Hashem's name in this world.

Part One

Making Every Moment Count

Chapter One

Utilizing Time

Wasting time is a form of partial death, a gradual suicide. Life, which consists of years, days, minutes, hours, and seconds, is the most precious possession we have. We need to learn how to utilize more efficiently this gift from Hashem.

> One moment of self-improvement and good deeds in this world is worth more than all of the World to Come.
>
> (Avos 4:17)

> We need to pray to Hashem to assist and enable us to avoid wasting time: "Teach us to count our days properly, so that we bring wisdom to our hearts" (Tehillim 90:12). All that we are today and everything we will become in the future are determined by the way we think and the way we use our time. Hashem has

divided time into days, months and years so that we notice its passing and utilize it more effectively.

(Rav Avigdor Miller, *Sing You Righteous*, p. 520)

✽ Would you like to be organized?

✽ Would you like to get more done in less time?

✽ Are your daily goals and objectives crystal clear and specific?

✽ Do you recognize that controlling how you spend your time will improve your life and increase your happiness?

You can become more productive!

This process can help you gain a promotion and a salary increase or an increase in income if you run your own business. It can help you feel more accomplished in your studies if you are a student and do more in less time if you are a homemaker. In addition, you will find that you have more time for Torah study, prayer, spending time with your family, and helping others.

How can we make the most of our time?

There are Torah guidelines for these timeless objectives. They apply to all of us, in every place and every era. Simply turn the page to begin.

Chapter Two

Clarity

The opening words of *Mesilas Yesharim* are "The foundation of devotion and the root of service [of Hashem] is to clarify...what is one's obligation in the world and what he must place his focus and direction on all the days of his life."

A person will always accomplish more when he has clear goals and objectives. We are taught, "In the path one is determined to go, he will be led" (*Makos* 10b). The key is self-awareness.

What do you really want to accomplish?

Do you desire to get to shul on time? To learn a certain amount daily? To give a certain amount to charity? To help another person with his needs? Clarify your goals and obligations in life.

What do you desire to achieve in each area of your life? What are the specific details? How do you plan to achieve it?

Each morning, it is worthwhile to clarify for yourself your most important goal or your two goals for the day. In this way, you will accomplish more each day and eventually change your life.

It is important to realize that how much time a person has for accomplishing his goals depends on how he uses the twenty-four hours of his day. Do you clutter your day with meaningless activities or do you spend it doing things that matter to you?

Rabbi Akiva would always say: "[Every person] is given the ability to choose" (*Avos* 3:19). You can choose how to spend your time and with whom to spend it, how to spend your money, and what to commit your emotional energy to. The power of choice is of critical importance!

We must realize that we are constantly making choices. Don't live your life on autopilot.

Whenever you say or think, "I have no time," you are actually saying, "Something else is more important to me now."

We make priorities in our minds all the time. When we stop to realize what we are choosing over what, we will find the time to do the things that are truly important.

Chapter Three

Priorities

Imagine that you are an expert at playing a certain children's game. You can spend a lot of time at it, you enjoy it immensely, and you are great at it. The only problem is that you happen to be thirty-seven years old, and you have no need for this type of activity.

To achieve, you need to concentrate on that which is of most value to your life and purpose! Our Sages teach us that the greatest mitzvah is Torah study (*Shabbos* 127a). A man is prohibited from leaving his learning unless he is confronted with another mitzvah which no one else can perform.

We need to constantly ask ourselves certain questions:

1. What is the most valuable use of my time right now?

Often we get caught up in a variety of meaningless tasks and forget about our main goals. Focusing on Torah study is essential. We must not let ourselves get distracted from this goal.

The Gemara teaches that Torah study leads us to the right actions (*Megillah* 27a). It will improve the quality of our life in every way. Although it may seem difficult to free up time for daily Torah study, it will ultimately be worthwhile. Torah study is the key to great success, achievement, respect, and happiness in life.

> *Minimize your involvement in other matters and involve yourself in Torah.*
>
> (*Avos* 4:10)

2. What activities can I cut back on, delegate to others, or discontinue in order to free up time for more important endeavors?

To have more time for learning, you have to stop using that time for other things. You will gain control of your time when you relinquish that which is less valuable and focus on that which is more important.

Your priorities change as you develop and

you have to adjust your schedule accordingly. Analyze your daily schedule carefully! We need the courage and the strength to stop doing the things that are no longer as important as they used to be.

Consider — what takes up most of your time? Can you do something more important in that time?

The key to success in life is positive action. We must clear away the negative and do only positive (*Tehillim* 34:15).

The next question to ask ourselves is

3. What can help me utilize my time and learn how to think better?

Make for yourself a mentor, and acquire for yourself a friend.

(*Avos* 1:6)

Your ability to learn from others is probably your most significant asset. "Who is wise? He who learns from every person!" (ibid. 4:1). If you listen and learn from others, you will benefit in every circumstance of life. By taking advantage of this skill you improve your ability to work in the most efficient manner possible.

Each of us has a unique combination of talents and skills that Hashem implanted in us. You were also blessed with teachers, relatives, and friends who can help you develop your skills so that you can reach your maximum potential. To get ahead in life we need to always keep learning, particularly from those around us.

If you feel you are not accomplishing your goals, ask those around you for advice. "How can I pray better? How can I learn Chumash, Mishnah, or Gemara with more insight, analysis, and creativity? How can I help my family members be happy?" You will never regret the time spent addressing these issues.

Chapter Four

Planning a Schedule

Why does the Torah say, "By the sweat of your *brow* you shall eat bread" (*Bereishis* 3:19), rather than "by the sweat of your hands" or "the sweat of your body"?

Rabbi Samson Raphael Hirsch explains that the Torah is teaching us to use our minds. If we think and plan ahead, we function more efficiently. A minute spent in planning may save you an hour wandering around without direction. When you are more organized and structured, you will accomplish more in less time and enjoy the process also!

Plan your goals, activities, and your thinking time so that you can accomplish more and benefit a greater return on your investment of mental, physical, financial, and emotional energy. Consider spending five minutes at the beginning of each hour to plan and five minutes at the end of each hour to review your accomplishments.

The Talmud (*Berachos* 32b) teaches that the great sages of old would spend an hour preparing for prayer and an hour thinking it over afterwards. Before prayer we need to consider our objectives: to praise and thank the Creator, to come closer to Him, and to ask Him for help. After praying, let us apply one of *Mesilas Yesharim*'s lessons for life and review two aspects of our behavior: 1) What we have done wrong, in order to improve, and 2) What we have done right, in order to continue and develop it more (*Mesilas Yesharim*, ch. 3).

By virtue of planning, you will prompt yourself to think more clearly and definitively about what you need to do.

"Fortunate is one who comes here [the World to Come] with his learning in hand" (*Bava Basra* 10b). The Maharsha explains that if one takes notes while learning it will help to concretize and solidify his learning and help him internalize it more. This method be applied to other aspects of life as well. Plan ahead. Think through your schedule with a pen and paper or the equivalent. Writing things down will help you be organized.

Of course, it takes discipline and self-control to plan ahead. But remember: "Who is strong? He who controls his inclination!" (*Avos* 4:1). Discipline yourself to plan the activities that you need to do. By prioritizing you will diminish your stress level, increase your productivity, and put your momentum to positive use.

Chapter Five

Time Investment

Often we resist putting time into a project, saying we're too busy for it and a superficial job will do just as well. This is a mistake. In *Pirkei Avos*, we are taught, "According to the difficulty, so is the reward" (*Avos* 5:23). The more time and effort we invest in a project, the better the results will be.

Look for ways to get better results. Try to serve Hashem with more effort and concentration and to do more than what you are being paid for, so to speak. Our Sages teach us to go beyond the requirements of the law, "*lifnim mishuras hadin*" (see *Chovos HaLevavos*, ch. 5). Go the extra mile in your learning, in helping another, and in whatever mitzvah comes your way.

Consider this most significant question:

Why did Hashem place me in the world in this particular era? What are the most important things that I do (or should be doing) daily? How can I do better?

Do your best to actualize your potential, to use your time wisely. The trick is not to be satisfied by merely doing more than others. Hashem expects you to do your best, which mean making sure that all you do is accomplished in the best way possible. If you focus on your learning, you may be able to learn through *Shas* one time, five times, ten times, or even one hundred times. When you commit yourself to excelling and achieving your potential, you will learn every lesson better.

Chapter Six

Time Choices

Put your hands on the wheel and steer it in the direction *you* desire. You can choose what to do, and in what order to do it. To a large extent, you are in control of managing your time. If you need to, you can stop the clock and change the sequence of events in your life.

"One mitzvah pulls another" (*Avos* 4:2). Once you get rolling with the first mitzvah, it will be easier to keep going. Almost as a reward for doing the right thing, Hashem sends you opportunities to do more of the same. You can choose to do certain things and thereby take control of situations.

How can we be certain of making the correct choices? We can begin by applying the lessons of the first *mishnah* in *Pirkei Avos*:

1. Be patient in making decisions. Don't rush into hasty decisions you may regret when the dust settles; instead, think about the potential consequences of your actions before you act.

2. Teach many people. Consider whether your actions will have a positive effect on those around you or a negative one. The more you do to influence others, the greater your time investment will be.

3. Made a fence around the Torah. This means that one should do his best to avoid pitfalls; stay away from places or actions which will cause problems and difficulties in your service of Hashem.

Keep these three lessons in mind whenever you need to make a decision or take action. Having patience, teaching others, and avoiding pitfalls are positive habits that we need to develop. We must practice these habits until they become our automatic reflexes.

Chapter Seven

Multiplying Your Time

When you learn Torah with a study partner you are more than doubling your time investment. Your combined efforts increase each person's brain power. Similarly, when you teach more people, you accomplish that much more. If you teach ten people, you are dramatically increasing your accomplishments and your impact on others.

Another way of multiplying your time is asking others for information. In this way you tap into their knowledge and experience, and you gain great wisdom in fulfillment of the *mishnah*, "Who is wise? He who learns from every person" (*Avos* 4:1).

You can change your life by approaching people who are successful in your line of work and asking them how they do this or that. They can give you plenty of advice. This is simple, obvious, and really works.

Review this *mishnah*, "Who is wise? He who learns from every person," at least a hundred times, and you will come to believe it. Then see how you can apply it on a daily basis.

Chapter Eight

Timeliness

"If not now, when?" (*Avos* 1:4). The great Hillel always repeated this saying, and it was a key factor in his tremendous success. The ability to act in a timely fashion is one of a person's greatest assets. If you can set priorities and achieve them with *zerizus* (alacrity), you will always succeed.

Life is short and we need to accomplish as much as we can. A righteous person does everything quickly (*Mesilas Yesharim*, ch. 5). He gets a lot more done in less amount of time. You can do the same. Don't waste time. When you are eager to serve Hashem, you will be more energized and accomplish more in less time.

Life is full of possibilities and opportunities. There are so many good things we can do. How-

ever, it is important to avoid becoming over-
whelmed. The Mishnah teaches: "You are not
obligated to finish the job, but neither are you
free to exempt yourself from it" (*Avos* 2:21). We
usually do not have enough time for all the jobs
we want to do. It is important to decide on your
priorities and do each task in a timely fashion.

Another key factor to getting things done on
time is setting deadlines. If you know there is
only a limited amount of time in which to complete the *masechta* you are learning, for example, you will avoid getting distracted by other
tasks or being caught up in conversations
which are not very important. Time is precious
and we must always use it wisely.

Chapter Nine

Become an Expert

The more you practice something, the better you become. In *krias Shema*, we say, "*Veshinantam levanecha*," which is explained by our Sages to mean, "Teach Torah in a sharp way" (*Rashi, Devarim* 6:7). We are instructed to teach Torah with constant review and analyses, so that it becomes fluent in our mouths. With practice and review, we can increase our output, our productivity, and our intellectual abilities.

We do not have enough time to become experts in everything, but there is enough time for what is most important. How can you utilize the talents and abilities Hashem has given you to make a real difference with your life? There is usually one activity in the realm of Torah and mitzvos that will be the best use of your time. Identify it and devote yourself to it wholeheartedly. You can be sure it is within your reach if you stay focused.

As we discussed in the last chapter, there will always be more to do. In order to truly develop, you need to prioritize: stop doing some things and begin to spend more time on Torah and mitzvos, the areas that will really make a difference in your life. Even if you select just one *mishnah* and review it one hundred times, you can alter the course of your life in a very positive way. Become an expert in one *mishnah*; your rewards will be immeasurable.

> *If you learned much Torah, you will be given great reward.*
>
> (*Avos* 2:21)

Chapter Ten

The Seven D's

Love Hashem, your God, with all your heart, all your soul, and all your resources.

(*Devarim* 6:5)

When you concentrate single-mindedly on maximum performance for Hashem, you will be most productive. You cannot do everything, but you can do one mitzvah at a time, step by step, and you can do it now. An hourglass keeps flowing, one grain at a time, until all of the sand passes through. You can do the same.

To sum up this program for change, we can keep in mind seven words that begin with "D."

❊ Desire — focus on truly wanting to attain your goals. Hashem will lead you there if your desire is solid (see *Makos* 10b).

✻ Decision — Make up your mind and heart; be firm about what you want.

✻ Discipline — Train yourself to listen and follow through consistently.

✻ Delegation — Ask others to assist you when you can't manage on your own.

✻ Determination — Never give up when faced with setbacks. "A tzaddik falls seven times, but he keeps rising" (*Mishlei* 24:16).

✻ Distance — Stay away from danger zones; put up fences to protect yourself from all spiritual hazards.

✻ Don't delay — Take action immediately; never fall into the bad habit of procrastination.

Part Two

Seize Every

Opportunity

Chapter Eleven

Seeking Opportunities

How does a person find opportunities in life? Does Hashem only present certain people with opportunities for good fortune? Shlomo HaMelech teaches us the secret to understanding this topic in *Sefer Mishlei*:

> *In front of an understanding person there is wisdom, but the eyes of a fool are to the ends of the earth.*

(*Mishlei* 17:24)

Hashem surrounds us with opportunities, but we need to learn how to notice and appreciate them. Just like fish in an ocean full of water, we live in a world full of air. This serves as a metaphor for us: Just as Hashem is constantly providing us with tons of air to breathe, He is also providing us with an abundance of other great opportunities for the taking.

We have been placed, thank God, in the right place at the right time. You are here! Seize the opportunity to do great things with your life. As we learned above, "If not now, when?" (*Avos* 1:14).

Now is the time for you to blossom. Hashem has made you with tremendous potential. You can call yourself the "super you." That is why the Mishnah (ibid.) says, "If I am not for myself, who will be for me?"

If you are not thinking, *Now is the time*, you may have missed the message, "You are the one." Take a good look at yourself. Notice your uniqueness and your immediate surroundings. Notice opportunities you may have been missing. Remember: "Every person has his time and every object has its place" (*Avos* 4:3).

Chapter Twelve

In Disguise

Many opportunities for greatness arrive in our lives disguised as hard work and challenges. They may not knock on your door, since opportunity only knocks when the bell is broken. Keep your ears open for bells that are ringing — otherwise you will miss the "visit" completely.

Some may call their hidden opportunity a problem. Others may call it a test. Shlomo HaMelech calls it "wisdom," as we saw in the previous chapter: "In front of an understanding person there is wisdom" (*Mishlei* 17:24). The key is to know that the solution is right in front of us.

Any difficulty we face successfully has become a step up on our ladder to perfection. How do we overcome our problems and utilize each opportunity that comes our way? Of course, we need Hashem's help to open our eyes to the answers that are right in front of us. We also need to be prepared to ask questions and learn from others.

Why is wisdom in front of an understanding person? *Metzudos* explains that this understanding person can learn from everyone around him. Every individual has lessons to teach you when you are ready to learn. Hashem positions people all around us throughout our lives, to teach us many lessons. If we open up our hearts and minds to learn from every person, we will gain immeasurably.

Don't spend too much time bemoaning your misfortune when you lose money on a business deal. View it instead as an opportunity for growth. It may not be easy to gain from the situation, but if Hashem sent this situation to you, He did so for a reason. You need to discover the reason and utilize it.

Chapter Thirteen

Torah Study

One of the greatest opportunities that awaits us is the mitzvah of Torah study. We need to commit ourselves to more regular, ongoing study with discipline and courage. As with other goals, the evil inclination is out to persuade us to stay away from intense learning programs. We are fooled into thinking, *How can I accomplish that much? Who do I think I am? It is just too difficult!*

Rashi explains the verse, "In front of an understanding person there is wisdom" (*Mishlei* 17:24), as follows: One should not say, "There is too much to learn, how can I ever manage it?" Rather, if he learns a small amount each day, he will accomplish great Torah goals. The wise method is to focus on the small amount for now, and watch it accumulate each day.

Always be on the lookout for small opportunities as well as big ones. A friend of mine told me the following story of an opportunity he discovered for making productive use of a negative situation. He was lying in bed one night, sleep eluding him. Suddenly he noticed the ticking of his alarm clock.

What is the purpose of that noise? he asked himself. He decided that he could utilize the clock's noise to review the basic mitzvah of loving Hashem. He mentally repeated the phrase "I love Hashem" numerous times with the ticktock of the clock until he fell asleep.

In the morning, he was amazed to see that he was totally relaxed and refreshed. He had a great morning, realizing that he could always use such situations to his benefit.

Chapter Fourteen

New Ideas

Many great inventions and discoveries were invented or discovered by people who focused on the opportunities which were right in front of them. As we learn in *Koheles* (1:9), "There are no new ideas." Most ideas are modifications and applications of old ideas. For example, tissues are disposable handkerchiefs. Airplanes are modeled after birds. Submarines are designed like fish.

Gold mines and diamonds can be found right in your backyard and in your office. Use the brain Hashem has blessed you with to discover new insights into life and new methods of doing things.

Learn how to think better. Improved thinking can help you grow and sustain profit. Learn from every new experience. Every mistake you make can be harnessed to your benefit.

If your mind is trained to look for new ways of doing things, you will gain immeasurably from life. Do you ever dream of getting paid to do something you love doing? It can happen if you put your mind to it. "In the path one is determined to go, he will be led" (*Makos* 10b).

Hashem is always setting things up for our benefit. If we develop a strong desire to accomplish positive goals, Hashem will guide us to accomplishing them. So pinpoint your goals and get ready to make changes in the way you do things.

Our imagination is an extremely valuable tool. "Who is wise? He who sees the future" (*Tamid* 32a). We need to think about the incredible opportunities that surround us and anticipate where they will lead us.

Activate your mind and heart by realizing that you are in Hashem's presence (*Shulchan Aruch* 1:1). He is the One and only One who has all the wisdom, power, and desire to assist us in achieving our goals in life.

When we develop an intense desire, invest concrete efforts, and combine them with serious prayers...Hashem creates the opportunities!

Chapter Fifteen

Dealing with Challenges

When you have a big problem on your hands, consider focusing on this thought: "The bigger the problem, the bigger the opportunity." This is based on a *mishnah*, "According to the difficulty, so is the reward" (*Avos* 5:23). Hashem has provided us with free will to choose how we react in life. In order to see how we take to making the right choices, He tests us with opportunities. Do we grab them with or without hesitation? Do we have the right priorities? We create our own opportunities to a certain extent by how we prepare ourselves to serve Hashem.

The three pillars of this world are Torah

study, prayer, and kindness (*Avos* 1:2). Do we focus on fulfilling our service to Hashem with enthusiasm? Every moment in life is an opportunity to thank Hashem!

> *Hashem saw everything He had made and behold it was very good.*
>
> (*Bereishis* 1:31)

We see Hashem's goodness over and over in the physical world. One scientific researcher discovered over three hundred practical uses for peanuts, including making beverages, soaps, and inks. He also made 118 products from sweet potatoes. We can learn from this about the infinite goodness in everything in Hashem's world.

If we recognize the goodness in the world, we will be propelled to a positive goal, to be flexible and creative, to be willing to change and consider new insights. We need to always improve ourselves and our methods of accomplishing on all fronts. We should always strive to provide quality service; to work smart, as well as hard; to communicate effectively; to accept responsibility; and to excel.

Chapter Sixteen

Goodness

Hashem is good to all.

(*Tehillim* 145:9)

This includes you! When you set out to be the best you can, with whatever you have, you will find more and more opportunities being sent your way by Hashem. It's not the job, it's *you!*

Everyone sees things differently. Do you find yourself facing a constant barrage of criticism at work? Don't view them as problems, but rather as a way to improve the quality of your work and learn from others. This is a key to growth in every industry. There are many ways to improve everything that you do. Learn from your customers. There are features and benefits that you do not realize in the products which you may think you know best.

It may be difficult to focus on Hashem's goodness if you are caught up in a maze of activities or surrounded by material objects. By simplifying your life, you will find yourself calmer and more aware of the goodness around you.

The matzos we eat on Pesach teach us the value of simplicity. Flour and water that is not enhanced by yeast or various flavors is sufficient to keep us alive. Similarly, many of the "extras" in our lives are unnecessary; we would be fine without them.

What are your priorities? Focus on spending more time on the important things. There are unlimited opportunities waiting for you in all directions, but which direction are you headed in?

Set goals and achieve them, no matter what job you may have now. It's not the job; it's how you look at it. Your horizons in life depend a lot on where your eyes are focused. With Torah goals, you will be assured of finding the right opportunities for your growth and advancement.

Part Three

Making the Most of
Your Work

Chapter Seventeen

Loving Work

"Love work" (*Avos* 1:10). This *mishnah* is an anchor for us as we strive to discover our calling in life. Make no mistake about it: "our calling" is surely a life of Torah study and mitzvah observance. But there is a principle that "If there is no food, there is no Torah" (*Avos* 3:17). We need some sustenance in order to learn.

Every person should discover the form of work that is right for him — something that interests him, suits his personality, and hits a chord deep within him. The Gemara teaches that each person has a profession that is beautiful in his eyes (*Berachos* 43b).

Why do we need to be instructed to love work? It's not always easy; we may occasionally be tempted to take a job that we will not enjoy. Sometimes we come to crossroads in life and we are scared. *Will my job pay the mortgage? Am I making the right choice?*

Was your company downsized, are you tired of your job, or were you fired? Are you trying to find merely any new job, or would you prefer to find yourself while you are at it? There may be a career waiting for you nearby, but you may not even realize yet that it is something for you.

"Love work" is a teaching we need to consider and relate to no matter what we do. It's easy to find just any job when you are determined to do so. But is it the right position for you? Is it the job that Hashem has assigned for you? You need to focus on your unique personal attributes. Try to see yourself in the big picture of Hashem's world.

Don't be afraid to try doing what you love and sticking to it through thick and thin (*Chovos HaLevavos, Shaar HaBitachon*). When you love your work, you will be able to overcome challenges. With the right attitude, you will merit Hashem's help.

When you make the best of every situation, Hashem helps you by making your situation better. Hashem is always leading you to where you need to be.

Chapter Eighteen

Developing a Love for Work

When you work hard at a job that doesn't interest you or work for others who demand work that you feel is unethical, immoral, or inappropriate, you get worn out quickly. How much money do you want to make and at what expense? You do need to sleep at night and to be happy with what you are doing.

Do you sometimes feel you really want a certain job that someone else holds? This type of desire could lead to jealousy, which you surely want to avoid. So let's rethink that desire. What you really want is to feel good about your job, just as you think someone else feels about his. You can achieve this goal if you work through the process step by step.

What will it take for you to love your work?

1. You need to make a minimum amount of money.

2. You want peace of mind.

3. You want to fit in with your working environment.

4. You want to have sufficient time left over to balance the rest of your life.

If you feel your present job does not meet these criteria, see what you can do to rectify the situation. Perhaps all you need is a change of attitude. Or maybe a more drastic change is needed — switching to a new job or even a new location.

The Gemara teaches that people have different feelings for different places and that sometimes moving to a new location can make a great difference (*Bava Metzia* 75b). You may be able to express yourself better and achieve more of your potential in a particular community, city, or country.

However, bear in mind that moving is not

the answer to everything. Bad habits and attitudes that you neglect to control will surface wherever you go. You must deal with them with wisdom, effort, and strategies.

If you do consider moving, take into account the following principle: "Move to a place of Torah" (*Avos* 4:14). Try to find the right environment for your spiritual growth.

Chapter Nineteen

A Positive Attitude

Some people change jobs every few years. They enjoy a job while they are learning new things, but then move on to another one when the first grows stale. This may be one form of fulfilling the *mishnah* to love your occupation. An even better way would be to develop your own inner enthusiasm.

Find your inner interest and free yourself to love what you do and grow with it. Tune into your inner song so that you can develop an ongoing appreciation for what you are doing.

Developing a positive attitude about yourself and what you do makes all the difference. You can also implement small changes to help you stay upbeat. For example, you can switch the position of your desk every few years or add pictures to the wall to refresh your mind.

You may feel that you are not making enough money to make ends meet. Instead of focusing on what you are lacking, try to change your attitude and elevate your thoughts! Think about the unlimited things you have to be grateful for; take responsibility for what you do and don't do.

> *One who has a merry heart will be at a constant party.*
>
> (*Mishlei* 15:15)

Your change of attitude will change the course of your life. Start today!

Chapter Twenty

Dealing with Others

When you interact with an employee at a company and he behaves in a courteous, warm, and thoughtful manner, doesn't it make a positive effect on your day? Doesn't a salesperson who treats you in a cheerful, respectful way make you happy?

Treat your boss, coworkers, employees, clients, and customers the way you yourself want to be treated. By loving your work you can positively affect others around you.

Whatever you do, your goal should be to satisfy your customers so that you will have a successful business which will make you happy. The best job in the world is one that makes others happy. Always try to excel at what you do in order to help people more and to help more people.

One should always be eager to meet new people so that he can have more people to love and help. "Love work" and "Love your friend as yourself" (*Vayikra* 19:18) go hand in hand.

One important thing to keep in mind is not to become a workaholic. You need to balance your love of work with everything else the Torah requires of you. For example, you also have to excel as a spouse and as a parent. One of our main goals in life is maintaining *shalom bayis*. If your wife feels she never sees you because you are always at the office, your marital harmony is bound to suffer.

In addition, when you deal with your children you should never try to get away with fulfilling the minimal obligation — make parenting one of your passions. Take pride in it. Keep your children in your plans and spend time with them because they are far more important than your work.

Chapter Twenty-one

Time to Relax

In addition to learning how to love our work, we also need to learn how to relax and take a break between projects. On the first verse of *Sefer Vayikra*, Rashi teaches the necessity of taking time to think between topics. Sometimes we need to release tension by breathing deeply, closing our eyes, stretching, or walking around.

The Gemara (*Kesubos* 111b) teaches that we should divide our time between walking, sitting, and standing. Even a short break can help you start fresh again. At times you may be rushing a bit, and your brain may begin to feel cluttered. It helps to take a break to relax. If you slow down, you will be able to think more clearly and work better.

Slowing down is also crucial for paying at-

tention to and hearing our inner selves. Our
bodies and minds need space in order to function efficiently and vigorously.

Try thinking of a way to perform your job
differently today. We are taught, "All your deeds
should be for the sake of Heaven" (*Avos* 2:12).
Consider how you can use your office, cubicle,
or workplace as a headquarters from which to
serve Hashem. Ask Hashem to help you increase your productivity and creativity.

"Rabbi Akiva says: 'Sing every day, sing every day' " (*Sanhedrin* 99a–b). Consider hum-
ming a tune periodically at work to make the
time pass more enjoyably. The tune can make
you more emotionally involved. Another option
is to listen to soft music. A tune may infuse us
with more enthusiasm and energy.

> *All those who sing in this world will merit to*
> *sing in the World to Come.*
>
> (*Sanhedrin* 91b)

We are in this world to learn how to sing to
Hashem. David HaMelech, "the sweet singer of Israel," says, "I am prayer" (*Tehillim* 109:4). His service

was to pour out his essence in song to Hashem, thus connecting to Him and clinging to Him always.

We all have to find those songs that we can excel at. You need to discover your inner voice, which you can transform into your song of life. Ask yourself: *What are the special gifts that Hashem blessed me with? Am I developing them properly? Am I utilizing them to connect with Hashem?*

Chapter Twenty-two

Passion and Commitment

Our thoughts fuel our passion and provide us with the courage to pursue our goals. Although it may seem difficult to become passionate about your work, it can be done. Passion is a choice. You can become more passionate about what you do when you focus on the possibilities it holds and the contributions you can make.

Decide to excel. Decide to overcome the odds. Excitement, determination, and commitment go together. Wake up each morning with passion for what you are going to do.

With patience, creativity, humility, persistence, and prayer you will be able to love your work. Do you like the thrill of creating things from scratch and seeing them develop? Do you like to make people happy? Do you like to provide a specific service? As you do these things each day, relish the opportunity to do the things you like best.

One of the benefits of enjoying your work is good health — you will have fewer colds, fewer headaches, and less indigestion. In addition, you will most likely sleep better at night and wake up energized.

You will certainly encounter many challenges in the course of your workday, but if you view each challenge as heavensent to help you grow and learn, it will not frustrate or upset you. "According to the difficulty, so is the reward" (*Avos* 5:23).

Commit yourself to learning from the many role models in the Torah and the Talmud. With these great people as guides, you will fuel your passion for work and your love for Hashem and people.

One of our greatest role models is Rabbi

Akiva, who began to dedicate himself to learning Torah at the age of forty and with time became the foremost sage of his generation. What steps did he take to become who he was? In *Pirkei Avos* (3:18) we have a list of some of the sayings he used to say regularly. Perhaps these are what inspired and motivated him to reach such great heights:

* ❋ "How beloved is man, who was created in Hashem's image."

* ❋ "How beloved are Israel, who are called Hashem's children."

* ❋ "How beloved are Israel, who have been given His most precious vessel [the Torah]."

Use Rabbi Akiva's example to inspire yourself to become the best person you can be. Be yourself, but be a better you. Learn who you are and what your strengths and abilities are. You are capable of doing things that others consider impossible if you trust in Hashem to help you succeed and keep praying to Him with hope and confidence.

Develop a sense of urgency for your mission

in this world. Don't worry about what you are not; focus on what you are. You are a unique creation, endowed with a mix of talents, abilities, dreams, and potential. We are taught, "Every individual is obligated to say, 'Hashem created the world for me' " (*Sanhedrin* 37a). Focus on this thought, and you will succeed!

Part Four

Forgiving

Chapter Twenty-three

Gaining Time

Anyone who forgives those who cause him pain will be forgiven for all his sins.

(*Rosh HaShanah* 17a)

What a powerful lesson! When you forgive others, Hashem forgives you, measure for measure. This principle can change our lives by releasing us from the prison of our sins.

Learn to release and cancel your negative feelings. Rashi on the above *gemara* explains, don't be exacting in measuring retribution to those who have wronged you. Let the insults pass by. We are instructed not to pass by a mitzvah, but we should always pass up the pain of hurt or embarrassment and practice forgiveness.

This principle will transform our lives. It will set us free from negative, draining emotions. Becoming sin-free is a very exciting, peaceful, and fulfilling experience. It is similar to the way we feel after a successful Yom Kippur. Your self-esteem, happiness, and energy will increase immensely.

Adopt the *mishnah*, "If I am not for myself, who will be for me?" (*Avos* 1:14), as your personal motto. Don't blame others for your problems; forgive them, forgive yourself, and move on.

People often walk around with grudges, resentment, bitterness, anger, and hatred. We know that "to love others as yourself" is a great mitzvah, one which is considered a foundation of the entire Torah (*Shabbos* 31a), but we tend to have many exceptions to the rule. We think that this particular person doesn't deserve our forgiveness.

If you find yourself in such a situation, it may be helpful to study the halachah in *Shulchan Aruch* (606:1) which states that one who refuses to forgive others is considered cruel. The *Mishnah Berurah*, in his note on this halachah (*Shaar HaTziyun* 8), adds that even if an antagonist was malicious and rebellious we should still forgive him, and Hashem will do the same for us!

When we fail to forgive others, when we choose to be critical and blame them, Hashem will blame us in like measure. Do we need that?

Failing to forgive others causes a tremendous drain of our energy, and thus of our precious time. Hashem wants us to be happy. He provided us with the guidelines to reach this objective, which we must learn and practice daily. The following chapters offer various guidelines to forgiving others, even when we find it difficult.

Chapter Twenty-four

Remembering

The key to developing the ability to forgive others who hurt us is choosing what to remember. We are cautioned in the Torah, "Beware not to forget Hashem" (*Devarim* 8:11), and "Remember Hashem, your God, for He is the One who gives you strength" (ibid., 18). Rather than remembering problems, difficulties, and dissatisfactions, focus on actively remembering the kindnesses Hashem bestows on you.

Remember that Hashem provided air for you to breathe when you woke up today and He continues to do so throughout the day. Your eyes are functioning. Your heart is beating and your mind is processing information. Say, "Thank You, Hashem, for being so kind to me!"

Memory is a very useful and beneficial tool. Fortunately, Hashem also created us with a delete mechanism. Forget unkind words. "Do not take revenge or bear a grudge against the people of your nation; love your friend as yourself" (*Vayikra* 19:18). The Rambam (*Hilchos Dei'os* 7:8) teaches that this attitude will promote the welfare of society and enable people to deal with each other successfully.

Although we may agree with the Rambam in theory, it is usually quite difficult to forget the wrongs others do to us. *Mesilas Yesharim* (ch. 11) teaches that this is very difficult for humans, since we are not angels, but it is a decree of our King that we must do our best to fulfill. He will assist us in accomplishing it.

The *Sefer HaChinuch* provides us with another tip to make the work of forgetting easier for us. In explaining the prohibition against taking revenge (mitzvah 241), it explains: "A person should focus on the fact that everything that happens to him, whether good or bad, is from Hashem, blessed is His name. Nothing happens without Hashem desiring it to happen. Thus, if someone causes a person pain or shame, he should realize that his sins have brought the decree of Hashem on him. Don't think of taking revenge on the person [who brought the pain], for it is not that person's fault."

Similarly, the Rambam (*Hilchos Dei'os* 7:7) teaches: "A person should always forgive others, for worldly matters are only silly issues.... Erase them from your heart."

> *Fortunate is one who remains silent and ignores even many insults. He will be spared one hundred evils.*
>
> (*Sanhedrin* 7a)

We learn from this that fulfilling this mitzvah is really for our own benefit! Of course, there are also benefits to the person you forgive, but there are many more benefits to yourself. You become energized, powerful, and closer to Hashem. You become more compassionate and more peaceful.

As you become a more forgiving, compassionate person, miracles will begin happening to you. New life will course through your veins. Your mind and heart will expand; your creativity and even your income can double and triple.

Chapter Twenty-five

Who's in Control?

One of our role models for the precious attribute of forgiveness is Yosef HaTzaddik. The Torah tells us his story in great detail, and there are many things we can learn from it.

After finally revealing himself to his brothers, Yosef "kissed all of his brothers and he wept over them" (*Bereishis* 45:15). The Shelah HaKadosh comments, "We learn how we should always forgive and pass over our *middos*. Although they had sinned against him, he cried and kissed them."

We may wonder, wasn't Yosef justified to hate his brothers, at least a little bit, for all the suffering they had brought on him?

When the brothers later asked Yosef for forgiveness, they said: "Forgive the sin of the servants of the God of your father" (ibid. 50:17). He was a true servant of Hashem, and they were also. On the mitzvah to "Love your friend as yourself" (*Vayikra* 19:18), the Talmud explains, "Love those who are your brothers in mitzvos" (*Sanhedrin* 86a). This love is actually an extension of the mitzvah to "love Hashem with all your heart" (*Devarim* 6:5), for it includes all those who love Hashem, His Torah, and His mitzvos. Thus, although the brothers had sinned, Yosef was still obligated to forgive them.

From Yosef's response to the brothers' request for forgiveness, we learn another lesson. He said: "Fear not; am I instead of Hashem?" (*Bereishis* 50:19). He did not deny their wrongdoing, but he did not punish them — even though he had the power to do so — because punishment is Hashem's prerogative. One may surely collect restitution through a *beis din* (a Jewish court of law), but beyond that we leave judgment to Hashem. The brothers themselves surely repented fully.

Yosef also said, "Hashem intended it for good" (ibid., 20). Hashem arranged Yosef's sale to eventually save the entire family from famine. As Rav Avigdor Miller, *zt"l*, teaches, "All seeming harm from people or nature inflicted upon the innocent is actually intended by Hashem for good" (*The Beginning*, p. 637). Hashem was manipulating all the events of the world for benevolent purposes.

Similarly, when we are wronged, we should view the situation as heaven-sent for our benefit. If the person who wronged you is a Torah-observant Jew, you are obligated to continue loving him, despite the wrongdoing. Leave the punishment to Hashem, as Yosef did. And remember that Hashem is behind the scenes, manipulating everything for our ultimate benefit.

Chapter Twenty-six

Secret to Longevity

The lesson, "Anyone who forgives those who cause him pain will be forgiven for all his sins," is found four times in *Shas*, *Rosh HaShanah* 17a, *Yoma* 23a, *Yoma* 87b, and *Megillah* 28a. It is applied to different situations for the many lessons we learn from it. The Rambam codifies these lessons in two places: *Hilchos Dei'os* 7:7 and *Hilchos Teshuvah* 2:10.

In *Hilchos Dei'os*, we learn to emulate Hashem's ways of kindness and compassion, to love others, not to hate, and not to be vengeful. In *Hilchos Teshuvah*, the Rambam gives the definition of complete repentance, which includes forgiving others "wholeheartedly and willingly." In the Rambam's words:

It is forbidden for a person to be cruel and to

refuse to forgive others. Be easily persuaded to forgive and consent to forgive wholeheartedly and willingly, even if one caused you much pain. This is the way of authentic Jews....

In *Megillah* 28a, we learn how to merit an increase in longevity: "Rabbi Akiva asked Rabbi Nechunya the Great: Which of your merits were the cause of your longevity?"

Rabbi Nechunya replies with three merits:

1. I never accepted gifts.

2. I forgave those who caused me suffering.

3. I was generous with my money.

The Gemara explains the second merit by quoting Rava's teaching: "Anyone who forgives those who cause him pain will be forgiven for all his sins," as we learn in *Michah* (7:18): "Hashem carries away the sins and passes over iniquity." This is interpreted, "Hashem carries away the sins of those who pass over iniquity."

In order to merit long life, we need to live in a manner which demonstrates that we are striving to utilize our time properly. When we refuse gifts in order to be independent and to be able to use our free will to grow, we lengthen our lives, as *Mishlei* (15:27) teaches: "One who hates gifts will live." Similarly, when we forgive others, we are freeing ourselves from pettiness and limitation. Since we are focusing on personal growth and not on ego, we deserve more life. So too, when we are flexible and generous with our money, helping others live more comfortably, we earn ourselves more life.

Chapter Twenty-seven

Shifting the Blame

*A person's foolishness corrupts his path, but he
blames Hashem.*

(*Mishlei* 19:3)

Some people constantly blame others for their failure. They often view themselves as victims of their past: "Did you know my parents? What do you expect from me?" "My siblings terrorized me!" They may blame others for their current inability to achieve: "My spouse is…" "My associates are…" We need to grow up and take responsibility for ourselves. The quality of your life depends on your behavior and your attitude — no one else's.

Forgive others. Let it pass, ignore, and forget, and you will begin to be happier, healthier, and more fulfilled. How do we fulfill the mitzvah to "love your friend as yourself"? By forgiving others, giving them another chance.

Blame is a form of anger. Why do we get angry with others? Many times we fail to give them the benefit of the doubt, to judge them favorably. Were they really out to get you? Maybe they didn't know better. Do we take the time (or make the time) to understand what the other person was going through and why he may have made an error?

Put an end to the past friction by following the teachings of our Sages! Forgive and move on. Life has so much to offer us, so many benefits that accrue to those who forgive others. Anger drains our energies. When we let go of anger from yesterday, we will be able to live today with positive energy and optimism. If you stop blaming others when things go wrong, your spouse will love you more and your boss may look upon you more favorably.

We get to choose how we think of our past and how we deal with the present and the future. It does take work to acquire this ability, but it is worth it. Ask a friend or a mentor to learn texts that deal with forgiveness (such as the *sefer Tomer Devorah*) with you.

> *One who judges others favorably will be judged favorably by Hashem.*
>
> (*Shabbos* 127b)

When we make peace and avoid dissension with others, Hashem does the same for us. For more on the topic of judging others, see our book *How to Judge Others* (Southfield, MI: Targum/Feldheim, 1995). This process may be the step we need to improve our lives and to merit the redemption, speedily in our time!

Part Five

Utilizing Life Properly

Chapter Twenty-eight

Productivity

As much as a person tries to make the most of his time, everyone must face the realization that his time on this earth is limited. The only thing that assures us eternal life is Torah and mitzvos. But we can buy more time on earth — and more Torah and mitzvos — by having children and disciples who perpetuate our name and continue in the path of Torah.

The Torah is replete with teachings on the importance of having children. Hashem's first command to mankind is "Be fruitful and multiply and fill the world" (*Bereishis* 1:28). Several parashiyos later, when Hashem promises Avraham that his reward is very great, Avraham's response is "What will you give me? I am childless" (ibid. 15:2). Avraham and Sarah lived with the primary goal of raising a nation that would serve Hashem (*Moreh Nevuchim* 3:51). This goal transcended all of their other desires in life.

The Talmud makes a dramatic statement:

> *Four are considered as deceased: a pauper, a leper, a blind person, and a childless person.*
> (*Nedarim* 64b)

Tosafos explains that one thing we learn from this statement is how much we need to pray for Hashem's mercy regarding these matters. Just as we must always pray that we should not become ill (*Shabbos* 32a) and that we should not suffer poverty (*Eiruvin* 41b), so too, we need to pray to Hashem to be blessed with children.

The Gemara's source for the status of a childless person is Rachel Imeinu's impassioned request of Yaakov: "Give me children; if not, I am dead" (*Bereishis* 30:1).

Avraham Avinu did not say, "I'm dead." Rather, he said, "Nothing is of value to me without children." Perhaps Avraham Avinu, who spent all his time teaching the world to serve

Hashem, justified his existence with that endeavor. All of the people he taught Torah were considered his children. But because the goal of having children is one of the greatest mitzvos a Jew can fulfill, Avraham felt that all the blessings he received from Hashem were insignificant in comparison to having his own children.

Chapter Twenty-nine

A Great Mitzvah

The mitzvah to procreate is the first mitzvah listed in the *Sefer HaChinuch*. The *Chinuch* describes it as a "great mitzvah" because through it we bring about the fulfillment of all other mitzvos in the Torah. The children who are born are the next generation that will fulfill the mitzvos.

This mitzvah is also emphasized by the prophet Yeshayah: "Hashem, the creator of Heaven and earth, has said: He did not create the world for emptiness, He desires it to be populated. I am Hashem; there is no other" (*Yeshayah* 45:18). *Tosafos* (to *Bava Basra* 13a and *Gittin* 41b) say this precept is a "*mitzvah rabbah*" (a great mitzvah).

In *Megillah* 27a, we are taught that one may

not sell a *sefer Torah*, even if he is in desperate need of funds, except for two mitzvos:

1. Torah study, which is precious because it leads to doing mitzvos, and

2. Marriage, because Hashem desires the world to be populated.

When *klal Yisrael* was in Egypt, the Torah teaches us, "The children of Israel were fruitful and they swarmed, increased, and became extremely mighty; and the land was filled with them" (*Shemos* 1:7). A few verses later, we are told, "As they were afflicted, so did they increase and spread" (ibid., 12).

The focus on increasing the Jewish people was the merit that brought about the redemption: "In the merit of the righteous women [who insisted on continuing to procreate], the Jewish nation was redeemed from Egypt" (*Sotah* 11b).

In addition, we are taught that this mitzvah is essential to hastening Mashiach's arrival:

> *Mashiach, son of David, will not come until all of the neshamos...will be born.*
>
> (*Yevamos* 62a)

King Chizkiyah was exceptionally righteous, yet the prophet Yeshayah informed him that he was going to perish — from this world and the next — if he continued to neglect the command "to be fruitful and multiply" (*Berachos* 10a). No matter how great is one's contribution to the world at large, if he chooses not to fulfill this mitzvah, he does not justify his right to live (Rav Avigdor Miller, *A Nation Is Born*, p. 14).

Chapter Thirty

Our Mission

Based on the command to "be fruitful and multiply and fill the world" (*Bereishis* 1:28), we are taught that it is incumbent upon us 1) to be fruitful, which means to have at least two children, a son and a daughter (*Yevamos* 61b); and 2) to multiply, meaning to have many more children, as many as possible, in order to "fill the world."

The Rambam codifies this mitzvah in the following way: "Even if one has already fulfilled the basic mitzvah of having children, he is still obligated by the laws of our Sages not to refrain from having more children as long as possible" (*Hilchos Ishus* 15:16). He adds: "Every increase of even one more child is like building a universe."

The Mishnah makes a remarkable statement: "The world was created only for being fruitful and multiplying" (*Gittin* 41b). We do not find such an expression used for any other mitzvah in all of *Shas*.

The mitzvah of bringing children into Hashem's world and providing them with the gift of life is a tremendous obligation and privilege, since children represent the future.

When the great matriarch Rachel was dying during her second childbirth, the midwife said to her, "Fear not, for this is also a son for you" (*Bereishis* 35:17). What type of message was this for a dying person?

Hashem designed this world as a place of preparation for the World to Come. The soul returns to Hashem at death, where it is to remain for eternity. This awareness is the true secret of life. It is the foundation necessary for choosing virtue over vice, for solving all of this world's mysteries, and for making life worthwhile (see *Mesilas Yesharim*, ch. 1).

Although Rachel was dying, she was informed that her life had been worth living, for she had produced another son who would per-petuate her merits for eternity.

Chapter Thirty-one

Dealing with Fears

Fulfilling the great mitzvah of having children is not always easy. The evil inclination has many weapons at his disposal to oppose our ways of virtue. He causes many fears and much confusion, distorting what is virtuous and filling us with doubts.

We need to invest all of our focus and efforts in overcoming this opposition.

What if a person does not make enough income to support a larger family? The answer is why should he have it in advance? Hashem will supply the extra provisions as they are needed. "As a child enters the world, his sustenance comes with him" (*Niddah* 31b).

Some people worry about how they will raise more children. The answer is "According to the difficulty, so is the reward" (*Avos* 5:23). Hashem does not send anyone challenges that he cannot handle. A test is always geared to the person's level, which only Hashem, our loving Creator, really knows.

Amram, the leader of the Jewish people in Egypt, felt that with the great suffering and the severity of the decrees, perhaps he should not bring any more children into the world. His daughter, Miriam, respectfully argued that by separating from his wife, Amram was making a decree more severe than that of the wicked Pharaoh, since Pharaoh had only decreed that baby boys be killed, while Amram was preventing both boys and girls from being born.

Amram was indeed great; he accepted her words and remarried his wife. They were then rewarded with a child who became the greatest prophet of all time, the leader who took the Jews out of Egypt and taught them the entire Torah, and the most humble individual who walked this earth — Moshe Rabbeinu!

When the *Shulchan Aruch* teaches the laws

of proper intentions for intimacy (*Orach Chaim* 240), the Tur states: "A person is obligated to spend time with his wife: 1) because he owes it to her as a requirement of the laws of *onah* (her time), 2) to fulfill the command of the Creator, and 3) to have children who will study Torah and fulfill mitzvos."

The Tur then quotes four levels of intention, all worthy of reward, from the Ravad:

1. For the sake of having children

2. To benefit the child

3. To provide for her needs

4. For his own needs

He then adds that the highest level of all is the first one, for the sake of having children.

The Rambam (*Hilchos Dei'os* 3:2–3) adds another point: "One should not be involved in these matters only for one's pleasure…. Rather, one should have in mind to gain health and strength in order to serve Hashem…. And to hope to have a son who may grow up to be a great Torah sage. One who follows this way will always be serving Hashem with all his actions...."

May we merit Hashem's assistance in this great mitzvah.

Part Six

Conquering

Time Limitations

Chapter Thirty-two

Eighteen Steps to Improving Your Life

A person will not acquire positive habits unless he learns them and practices them. It takes decision, discipline, and determination. If you follow the Torah's teachings in these areas, you will become more productive, effective, and efficient. These steps will help you achieve your goals.

Step One

On the path one is determined to go, he will be led.

(*Makos* 10b)

The five basic steps to goal setting are

✱ Decide exactly where you are going

✲ Make sure it's what you really want

✲ Set deadlines

✲ Plan your steps

✲ Begin

Think about and review your goals daily. Do something every day to act on your goals.

Step Two

A wise person looks ahead.

(*Tamid* 32a)

Plan each day and each hour ahead. When you daven *shacharis*, pray for your needs of the day until *minchah*. At *minchah* pray for your needs until *maariv*, at *maariv* pray for your needs until the following morning's prayer.

Step Three

What is the best path for life?... He who fore-sees the future.

(*Avos* 2:13)

Evaluate and predict the consequences of your actions as you go through your day. Time keeps moving. Use it wisely.

Step Four

The *Mesilas Yesharim* (ch. 3) teaches that one should spend time every day deciding which activities take priority. Avoid activities of little value. Focus on the significant and most valuable activities. Strive to really make a difference.

Step Five

Our primary task in the world is to learn Torah. Unless one encounters a mitzvah which cannot be done by others, he should not stop learning.

The Mishnah teaches, "Reduce your other involvements and be involved with Torah" (*Avos* 4:10). Say no to things that are not so important. Delegate or eliminate tasks to free up time for that which really counts.

Step Six

Where do you need to improve? What skills do you need to develop better? There are many skills that you can improve if you focus on them.

Always try to upgrade and sharpen your

skills. Whatever you do best, you can do even better if you keep learning how to improve on it. You can become more knowledgeable and competent in your field. You can decide to become better at what you do!

Step Seven

Consider what is your weakest point. What seems to limit your growth? Concentrate on improving yourself in that specific area.

Many of the obstacles you face may be internal. Ask yourself, "What is in me that is holding me back?"

Step Eight

What do you do well? What do you enjoy most? Use your special talents to make a significant contribution to the world around you.

Step Nine

If I am not for myself, who will be for me?
(*Avos* 1:14)

In other words:

✳ What are *my* most important activities?

✻ What can I — and only I — do that makes a difference?

✻ What is the most valuable use of my time right now?

✻ "If not now, when?"

We need to keep asking ourselves these questions over and over again.

Do first things first — and cancel the second things.

Step Ten

Studies have determined that taking off one full day every week can change your life dramatically. For this day you should avoid all forms of work. You should spend time with your family, relax, take walks, and allow your brain and body to recharge themselves. Use Shabbos properly!

Step Eleven

In order to maintain your daily energy level, be sure to eat some bread every morning for breakfast. A high energy level is vital for a high level of production, more happiness, and greater success. Take action to guard your health, as required by the Torah.

Step Twelve

The Talmud teaches us to consider the possibility that we may have only one day left on this earth (*Avos* 2:15 and *Shabbos* 153a). What do you want to accomplish before your life is over? Learn to set deadlines for yourself.

Step Thirteen

You can finish the whole *Shas* in seven and a half years if you do one *daf* a day. You can become healthier by eating a little less and exercising a little more, day after day. One step at a time is the secret to accomplishing great goals.

Challenge yourself to improve and excel. Choose to be a "*lifnim mishuras hadin*" person (one who goes beyond the minimum requirements of the Torah law). Start a little earlier, stay a little later, and work a little harder. You will begin to enjoy life more.

Step Fourteen

Coach yourself and encourage yourself as if

the great sages were speaking to you. Hillel would say to you, "If not now, when?" (*Avos* 1:14). Rabbi Akiva says, "Sing every day" (*Sanhedrin* 99b). Nachum Ish Gam Zu would say, "This, too, is for good" (*Taanis* 21a). David HaMelech says, "Serve Hashem with joy" (*Tehillim* 100:2). In *Ashrei*, he teaches, "Hashem is good to all" (*Tehillim* 145:9). These are just some examples of the many sayings you can adopt to transform your life.

Step Fifteen

Who desires life, who loves days to see good?
(*Tehillim* 34:13)

Always look for the good in every situation. Every setback has a valuable lesson. Always look for solutions. Think positive — Hashem is in control and He is good to all.

Step Sixteen

Divide your most difficult task into small sections and focus on just one section at a time. Once you accomplish that, the next section will be much easier. Each small step energizes you for the next step. You can write a book by resolving to write one page or even one paragraph every day, until you finish.

> *When you grab hold of a small amount, you will succeed.*
>
> (*Sukkah* 5a)

Step Seventeen

> *Establish fixed times for your Torah learning.*
> (*Avos* 1:15)

Set aside a specific time of day for your Torah study. This rule can be applied to many other things as well. The key is to plan your day in advance with time slots for every task. Each task is then accomplished, one at a time.

An uninterrupted time block can do wonders. You will find it easier to finish your job in half the time. Organize your schedule so that you can concentrate on your tasks at specific times!

Step Eighteen

Now is the time. Take action, rather than talking about what you plan to do (see *Avos*

1:15). "The lesson is not as essential as the action" (*Avos* 1:17). Develop a sense of urgency (*zerizus*) in order to do things quickly and well. The faster you work, the more energy you will have.

With Hashem's help, you will succeed!

Small Books.

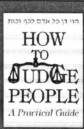

TARGUM PRESS Books

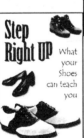